What Is Happening To Our Children?
What Happened To The America I Grew up In?
Being Destroyed From Within
Volume 3
By Ann Marie McKay

What Is Happening To Our Children?
By Ann Marie McKay

Prologue

Sadly, it took a tragedy to end my writer's block that I had been going thru. I had been feeling discouraged because my books weren't selling unless I offered them for free. I had received a negative review about one of my books and someone had gotten angry about one that was based on a time that really happened in my life though no names of existing people were used in the story.
While I do not think I'll ever get rich from my writing(It would be nice.) and the main goal is to share my writing and maybe touch hearts or open minds to different perspectives it is great when someone buys a book.
So there I was thinking maybe I should give writing up. Then on February 14,2018 the school shooting happened in Florida. As I watched the faces of the victims being shown on television and heard the stories of these beautiful young people who were high achievers and had such plans and dreams for the future it broke my heart.
I remembered how it was when I was growing up and going to school. The first shooting I was aware of was November 22,1963 when President Kennedy was killed. I started wondering about school shootings. When was the first one? Were there school shootings in the past? Why are there so many more now? The research began and here are my findings.
This book has more then one part. While part 1 is about school shootings, part 2 is about child abuse and neglect in homes. Part 3 compares the past to now. What's changed? What do we need to change to protect our children?
I do not expect my readers to agree with all or any of my views but perhaps if we all decide to get some changes made our children will once again be able to be safe in their homes and in their schools.

God bless all.
Sincerely,
Annie

Table Of Contents

Part 1

Chapter 1
History Of School Shootings

18th Century: ONE school shooting

19th Century: 28 school shootings

20th Century: 227 school shootings

21st Century: 227 school shootings before 2018

These numbers were found during my research. While trying to be as exact as possible there is always a chance of error.

The 18th Century

July 26th, 1764
Pennsylvania

Indians attacked a school and shot the teacher. 9 or 10 children were killed or injured. Other weapons were used upon the children instead of guns.

The 19th Century

November 12th, 1840
Charlottesville, Virginia

A Law Professor was killed by a student.

November 2nd, 1853
Louisville, Kentucky

A student shot a school master in an act of revenge. He had punished the boys brother excessively the day before. The student was acquitted.

August 16th, 1856
Florence, Alabama

A school master strangled a student. The boys father shot the school master in an act of revenge.

July 8th, 1858
Baltimore, Maryland

The 15 -year -old son of the Baltimore Marshall of Police was killed during Sunday School.

April 30th, 1866

An editorial in the New York Times argued against students carrying pistols.

June 8th, 1866
New York City
Public School 18

13- year- old brought a pistol to school. He shot and injured a classmate.

December 22, 1868
Chattanooga, Tennessee

A boy who refused to be punished left school. He returned the next day with his brother
 and a friend seeking revenge. Upon not finding the teacher at the school they went to
his home where a gun battle occurred. 3 died, only the brother survived.

March 9th, 1873
Salisbury, Maryland

1 dead. The shooter later committed suicide.

May 24th, 1879
Lancaster, New York

At a girl's school, the telegraph operator shot and injured the Superintendent of the
stables as a carriage loaded with female girls pulled out of the stables.

March 6th, 1884
Boston, Massachusetts
Boys imitating "Jesse James" held a meeting at school. The gang ran as police officers
approached. One fired at the officer but missed. 2 of the boys were caught. The rest
escaped among them the one that did the shooting.

March 15th, 1884
Gainsville, Georgia

Some very drunk farmers left a tavern drinking and shooting. They fired at the front door of a girl's school. No one was hurt.

July 4th, 1886
Charleston, South Carolina

At a Sunday School meeting a girl shot and killed a boy for "circulating slanderous reports" even though her brother had fought and whipped him days before.

April 12th, 1887
Water town, New York

A student at Potsdam Normal School committed suicide by shooting himself in the head.

June 12th, 1887
Cleveland, Tennessee

A boy shot and killed teacher for whipping his little sister the day before.

June 13th, 1889
New Brunswick, New Jersey

A man upset over an argument with a school trustee, went to a window and fired a pistol into a school room. The bullet went into the wall just above the teacher's head.

April 9th, 1891
Newburgh, New York

1st known mass shooting occurred when a 70 year old man fired a gun at a group of students playing in the yard at St. Mary's Parochial School. There were several students injured.

20th Century

There were not many reports of mass shootings during the first 3 decades of the 20th Century. The 3 most violent attacks involved arson or explosives.

February 26th, 1902
Camargo, Illinois

A male teacher shot and killed a female teacher for refusing to marry him. He also shot at a student who tried to help and wounded himself in a failed suicide attempt. When an angry group came to hang him, he ran out of the school. Then he grabbed a shot gun from a farmer and again shot himself. He then ran and jumped into a well where he eventually drowned.

February 24th, 1903
Inman, South Carolina
Inman High school

17- year- old student was shot and killed by a teacher after he resisted punishment. The teacher claimed the student struck the pistol he had drawn in self- defense and it accidentally went off. He was acquitted of murder.

October 10.1906
Cleveland, Ohio
South Euclid School

A man shot and killed a 22- year -old teacher. He later committed suicide.

March 23rd, 1907
Carmi, Illinois

A man shot and killed another at a school house because of a remark he made about the man's daughter.

March 11th, 1908
Boston, Massachusetts

A woman was shot and killed by another woman at a finishing school in Boston.
She then committed suicide.

April 15th, 1908
Asheville, North Carolina

A man shot and killed his daughter at Normal and Collegiate Institute. He then killed himself.

February 12th, 1909
San Francisco, California

A student was killed as she arrived at her school. The shooter then attempted and failed to kill himself.

January 10th, 1912
WarrenVille, Illinois

Man shot and killed a teacher for refusing his advances. Then he shot and killed himself. It happened at the school house after the students had been dismissed for the day.

March 27th, 1919
Lodi Township, Michigan

19 year old teacher shot and killed in school.

April 2nd, 1921
Syracuse, New York

A professor killed the Dean in his office then committed suicide.

May 18th, 1927
Bath, Michigan
Bath Consolidated School
Deadliest Act of Mass Murder at a school at this time.

School Treasurer killed his wife. He also destroyed his house and barn. He then blew up the school. The explosion killed 38, mostly children. The dynamite was located in the basement of the school. He pulled up to the school in his car to fire one shot setting off the dynamite. He then blew up the car, killing himself and 4 other people.

The 1930s
February 15th, 1933
Downey, California
Gallatin grammar School

A doctor shot and killed his wife and 8 year old son. He also fired 3 more shots at another son. He then committed suicide. His wife who was a teacher had filed for a divorce.

September 14th, 1934
Gill, Massachusetts
Northfield Mount Hermon School
A Headmaster killed by a shotgun blast through the window. The murder was never solved.

December 12th, 1935
New York City, New York

School of Dental & Oral Surgery Lab worker shot and killed 2 professors and wounded a doctor at Columbia Presbyterian Hospital then killed himself.

April 27th 1936
Lincoln, Nebraska

A professor shot and wounded another professor at University of Nebraska. He tried to escape but was surrounded by campus police. He then killed himself.

June 4th, 1936
Bethlehem, Pennsylvania

A student shot and killed his English teacher for refusing to change his grade to a passing one. Then he committed suicide.

September 24th, 1937
Toledo, Ohio
Arlington Public School

A 12 -year- old shot and wounded the principal because she refused to call a schoolmate when the 12 -year- old requested she do so. He then ran from the school grounds and shot and wounded himself.

The 1940s
May 6th, 1940
Pasadena, California

After being fired as the principal of South Pasadena Jr, High School, a man shot 6 school officials. He killed 5, wounded 1 then shot himself in a suicide attempt.

May 23rd, 1940
New York City, New York
Dwight Schools For Girls

The janitor of the school shot and wounded the secretary.

July 4th, 1940
Valhalla, New York

A father angry by his 15 -year -old daughter's refusing to leave boarding school and return home visited the school where he shot and killed her.

September 12th, 1940
Uniontown, Pennsylvania

29- year- old teacher shot to death inside 3rd grade classroom. Man then shot himself in the chest. He was already married but courting the teacher who had ended the relationship when learning he was married.

October 2nd, 1942
New York City, New York
William J. Gaynor Jr. High School

Math teacher was shot and killed by a student.

February 23rd, 1943
Port Chester, New York
Harvey School

13 -year- old fatally shot himself.

June 26th, 1946
Brooklyn, New York
Public School 147 annex of the Brooklyn High School for Automotive Trades

A 15 year old was shot in the chest by a gang that wanted his money.

November 24th, 1946
New York City, New York
St. Benedict's Parochial School

13 year old shot & killed himself while watching a school play.

December 24th, 1948
New York City, New York

An accidental shooting occurred when a 14 year old was fatally wounded by a
17 year old during target shooting. The shooting involved a .22 caliber rifle.

March 11th, 1949
New York City, New York
Stuyvesant High School

16 year old accidentally shot in the arm by a classmate who had a pistol in the
classroom.

November 19th, 1949
Columbus, Ohio
Ohio State University

A freshman grabbed a .45 caliber hand gun and shot and killed his fraternity brother.
The deceased was an Ohio State Senior.

<u>1950's</u>
July 22nd, 1950
New York City, New York
P. S. 141

16 year old shot in wrist and stomach at a dance.

November 27th, 1951

A 15 year old was fatally shot as fellow students watched.

April 9th 1952
New York City, New York

15 year old shot a dean at a boarding school over having pin up pictures of girls wearing bathing suits. The dean wanted them removed.

July 14th, 1952
New York City, New York
Columbia University American Physical Society

Student killed secretary with a .22 caliber pistol.

September 3rd, 1952
Laurenceville, Illinois
Lawrenceville, High School

Man shot and killed 25 year old librarian after she had ended their engagement.

October 2nd, 1953
Chicago, Illinois
Kelly High School

14 year old shot to death by 14 year old girl after he handed her a gun and dared her to pull the trigger. He claimed the gun was "only a toy." Coroner's jury ruled the shooting was an accident.

October 8th, 1953
New York City, New York
Machine & Metal Trades High School

17 year old student shot and wounded while looking at handmade pistol by another student.

May 15th, 1954
Chapelhill, North Carolina
Phi Delta Theta House
University of North Carolina

After all night party one student took out a gun and started shooting in his fraternity bedroom. His roommates were wounded and he was shot and killed.

January 11th, 1955
Swarthmore, Pennsylvania
Swarthmore College

After some roommates urinated on his mattress a 20 year old returned with a shotgun and killed one of his fellow students.

April 17th, 1956
Bronx, New York
Bronx Vocational School

A 16 year old shot and killed an 18 year old because of an argument over a basketball.

May 4th, 1956
Prince George's County, Maryland
Maryland Park Jr. High School

15 year old shot and fatally wounded 1 teacher and injured 2 others.

October 20th, 1956
New York, New York
Booker T. Washington Jr. High School

A student was wounded by another student with a home made weapon.

October 2nd, 1957
New York City, New York

A 15 year old shot a 16 year old in the leg at a city high school.

May 1st, 1958
Massapequa, New York
15 year old was shot and killed by a classmate.

September 24th, 1959
New York
Morris High School

27 men & boys and an arsenal were seized in the Bronx, Police stopped a gang war
after a teenager was shot and killed at Morris High School.

<u>1960's</u>

February 2nd, 1960
Hartford City, Indiana
William Reed Elementary School

Principal shot and killed 2 teachers using a shotgun. Then he fled into a forest where he committed suicide.

June 7th 1960
Blaine, Minnesota

40 year old mailman shot to death a 33 year principal with a .12 gauge shotgun.

April 20th, 1961
Chicago, Illinois
Lewis-Champlain Elementary School

Teacher sexually assaulted and stabbed to death by a 14 year old. He was convicted and sentenced to 55 years in prison.

October 17th, 1961
Denver, Colorado
Morey Jr. High School

A 14 year old got into an argument with a 15 year old. He pulled out a.38 caliber revolver and wounded the boy. A stray bullet hit a 14 year old girl who later died from the wound.

August 1st, 1966**
University of Texas-Austin

Man killed 16 and wounded 31 others during a 96 minute shooting rampage.

November 12, 1966
Mesa, Arizona
Rose-Mar College of Beauty

18 year old took 7 people hostage. he made them lie down in a circle on the floor.
 He then shot them in the head with a.22 caliber pistol. 4 women and a 3 year old died. 1 woman and baby were injured but survived. Man was arrested by police.

January 20th, 1968
Miami, Florida
Miami Jackson High School

16 year old girl killed a fellow student also a 16 year old girl. The shooter was reportedly threatened with a razor by the victim during an argument and stated the gun went off accidentally during the struggle. A.22 caliber pistol was used.

February 8th, 1968
Orangeburg, South Carolina
South Carolina State University

200 student protesters gathered on campus to protest segregation of the All Star Bowling Lane. that night they started a bon fire.
As police attempted to put out the fire one was injured by a piece of banister thrown. The police believed they were being attacked by small weapons fire. They then fired into the crowd killing 3 and wounding 27 others.

May 17th, 1969
Los Angeles, California
University of California

2 members of Black Panther Party fatally shot during a meeting. The shooter escaped but 3 others were arrested in connection with the shooting.

November 19th, 1969
Tomah, Wisconsin

14 year old boy shot principal to death with a .20 gauge shotgun.

1970's

May 1970*****
Police opened fire on Jackson State University Campus.
National guard opened fire on campus of Kent State University.
 Also happened May 1970.

<u>Mid to Late 1970's</u>
considered 2nd most violent period in U. S. school shooting history.

December 30th, 1974
Olean, New York

17 year old armed with a rifle and a shotgun killed 3 adults and wounded 11 others at his high school which was closed for the Christmas holidays. He was a "loner" and kept a diary which told of several "battle plans" for attacking the school.

June 12th, 1976*****
California State University
Fullerton Massacre

School custodian used a <u>semi automatic rifle </u>in the library killing 7 and wounding 2.

February 22nd, 1978
Lansing, Michigan

15 year old killed 1 and wounded a second with a <u>Luger pistol.</u>

January 29th 1979
Grover Cleveland Elementary School
California

16 year old girl used a rifle to kill and wound 9.

<u>1980's</u>

January 20th, 1983
St. Louis County, Missouri
Parkway South Middle School

An eighth grader brought a bag containing 2 pistols and a murder/suicide note to school. He was in the study hall classroom when he opened fire. 1 student was fatally shot in his stomach. The 2nd received a non fatal wound. The shooter then committed suicide. He was angry over comments being made about his brother.

<u>September 1986-September 1990*****</u>
<u> 71 killed by guns at schools.</u>
<u>201 severely wounded.</u>
<u>242 held hostage at gunpoint.</u>
<u>Late 1980's saw a major increase in school shootings.</u>

September 4th, 1985
Richmond, Virginia
East End Middle School

12 year old boy shot a girl. he used his mother's gun.

October 18th, 1985
Detroit, Michigan
homecoming football game

A boy who had been in a fight earlier in the day, shot and injured 6 students with a shotgun.

November 26th, 1985
Spapaway, Washington
Spapaway Jr. High School

14 year old girl used a .22 caliber rifle to kill 2 boys and commit suicide.

December 9th, 1985
Philadelphia, Pennsylvania
Archbishop Ryan School For Boys
22 year old mentally ill patient took 6 students hostage. No one was hurt.

December 10th, 1985*****
Portland, Connecticut
Portland Jr. High School

Principal locked a 13 year old boy inside an office after a heated discussion. The
boy pulled out a 9 mm assault rifle and started shooting. The glass door was shattered
and struck the forearm of the secretary and injured the principal. The boy then ran to
the 2nd floor and shot the janitor in the head and took a student hostage. Members
of his family came to the school and talked to him over the intercom. after 45 minutes
he tossed the gun out a window and surrendered. He was then taken into custody.

May 16th, 1986
Cokeville Elementary School Hostage Crisis*****

2 people in mid 40's took 150 students and teachers hostage. They were demanding
300 million dollars ransom. the woman set off a bomb accidentally killing herself and
injuring 78 students. The man wounded a teacher attempting to run then committed
suicide.

March 2nd, 1987
An honor student 12 years of age killed himself and a classmate.

May 20th, 1988
Winnetka, Illinois

30 year old killed 1 boy, wounded 5 others at an elementary school. She then took a
 family hostage and shot one man. Then she committed suicide.

September 26th, 1988*****
Greenwood, South Carolina
Oakland Elementary School

19 year old shot and killed 8 year old girl and wounded 8 other children using a 9 round
.22 caliber pistol.

When he went into the girls bathroom to reload he was confronted by a Physical Education Teacher who he shot in her hand and mouth. then he went into a 3rd grade classroom and wounded 6 more students.

December 16th, 1988
Virginia Beach, Virginia
Atlantic Shores Christian School

Boy 15 used a <u>SWD Cobray M-11 semi automatic pistol</u> on his teachers. He struck a teacher in the arm. When she fell down he killed her. He then injured a man. When he turned the gun on his classmates it jammed and another teacher stopped him before he could continue firing.

January 17th, 1989*****
Cleveland School Massacre
Stockton, California

5 school children killed, 29 wounded. A gunman fired over 100 rounds into a school yard with a <u>AK47.</u>

<u>The 1990's</u>

<u>From the late 1980's to the early 1990's there was a large increase in gun violence in the schools.</u>

<u>1998-1999</u>
<u>3,523 students were expelled for bringing a fire arm to school.</u>

May 1st, 1992
Olivehurst, California

20 year old killed 4 and wounded 10 at his former high school. The attack was revenge for getting a failing grade.

The late 1990's saw a major reduction in gun related school violence. Did the 1994 Federal Assault Weapons Ban perhaps contribute to the lower numbers?

October 12th, 1995
Blaceville, South Carolina

A suspended student used a .32 caliber revolver to shoot 2 Math teachers.

November 15th, 1995
Lynnville, Tennessee

17 year old boy with a .22 caliber rifle shot and killed a student and a teacher.

February 2nd, 1996
Moses Lake, Washington
14 year old opened fire on algebra class. 2 students and 1 teacher were killed with 1 other wounded.

February 19th, 1997
Bethel, Alaska

16 year old boy killed a principal and 1 student. 2 others were wounded.

October 1st, 1997
Pearl, Mississippi

A boy 16, rumored to be a Satan worshiper, killed 2 students and wounded 7. He was also accused of killing his mother.

December 1st, 1997
West Paducah, Kentucky
Heath High School

A 14 year old freshman killed 3 and wounded 5 students participating in a prayer circle. He pleaded guilty but mentally ill and was sentenced to life in prison with eligibility for parole in 2023.

December 15th, 1997
Stamps, Arkansas

A 14 year old hiding in the woods shot and wounded 2 students standing in the parking lot.

March 24th, 1998
Jonesboro, Arkansas
Westside middle School

After pulling a false fire alarm a 13 year old and 11 year old in the woods shot at teachers and classmates. 4 students and 1 teacher were killed 10 others were wounded. The boys were convicted of murder and sentenced to jail until they turn 21.

April 24th, 1998
Edinboro, Pennsylvania
James W. Parker Middle School

1 teacher killed. 2 students wounded at a dance. a 14 year old was charged.

May 21,1998*****
Springfield, Oregon
Thurston High School

15 year old arrested and released for bringing a gun to school. he returned the next day and killed 2, wounded 22 others in the school cafeteria. His parents were found dead in their home. He was sentenced to 112 years in prison.

June 15th, 1998
Richmond, Virginia

14 year old wounded a teacher and a guidance counselor in the school hallway.

April 20th, 1999*****
Littleton, Colorado
Columbine High School

 An 17 year old and an 18 year old plotted for over a year how to kill at least 500 and blow up their school. During a 1 hour rampage they shot and killed 17 students and 1 teacher. 21 others were wounded. The boys committed suicide.

May 20th, 1999
Conyer, Georgia
Heritage, High School
15 year old injured 6 students.

<u>**The 21st Century**</u>
Between the 1999 Columbine Shooting until the December 14th, 2012 mass shooting at Sandy Hook Elementary School at least 31 school shootings took place. Did the fact that the 1994 federal ban on Assault Weapons expired in 2004 and was not renewed help lead to the increase of school violence?

September 24th, 2003
Cold Springs, Minnesota
Rocori, High School

15 year old pulled a pistol out of his gym bag and shot and killed 2 students.

March 21st 2005
Red Lake, Minnesota
Red Lake Reservation

16 year old used a shotgun to kill his grandfather and the grandfather's girlfriend. He then went to the high school where he killed a security guard, teacher and 5 students. 5 others were injured. He committed suicide in an empty classroom..

October 6th 2006
Nickel Mines, Pennsylvania
Amish School House

32 year old took 10 girls hostage. As police came to the building, he shot 10 killing 5 of the girls. The children's ages ranged from 6 to 13. The shooter committed suicide.

April 16th, 2007
Blacksburg, Virginia
Virginia Polytechnic Institute & State University

In 2005 a **Montgomery County Judge** found the person who ended up becoming one of the deadliest school shooters in U. S. history mentally ill and a danger to himself. He was found to have a severe anxiety disorder yet passed 2 background checks because at the time Virginia did not require ALL mental health records to be submitted to the National Instant Criminal Background Check System. On April 16th, 2007 now a senior and an English major the shooter armed with 2 pistols and dozens of rounds of ammunition shot and killed 32 and wounded 17 in 2 separate attacks taking place on campus hours apart from one another.
The shooting did encourage many states including Virginia to update mental heath reporting by submitting other records besides mental incompetency or hospitalization court ordered to the NICS.

February 8th, 2008
Baton Rouge, Louisiana
Louisiana Technical College

23 year old woman using a 357 revolver killed 2 then herself.

February 14th, 2008
Dekalb, Illinois
Northern Illinois University

27 year old wearing a t -shirt with the word "terrorist" over a picture of an assault rifle went to the university with 3 handguns, a shotgun and a knife. He also had a utility belt with 2 magazine holsters, a handgun holster, 8 loaded magazines. He was on the stage of the school auditorium and exhausted his shotgun rounds firing upon students. He then walked up and down the aisles using a **9mm clock pistol.**
He killed 5 people and wounded 21 then took his own life.

February 27th, 2012
Chardon, Ohio
Chardon High School

A student killed 3 and injured 3 others. In the courtroom he showed no regret and was sentenced to 3 life terms.

April 2nd, 2012 *****
Oakland, California
Oikos University
Korean Christian School

43 year old former student interrupted a nursing class and ordered the classmates to line up against the wall. He had a **.45 caliber semi-automatic handgun,** using it he killed 7 and wounded 3.

Since 1982 there have been at least 61 mass murders. Rate of people killed in the United States by gun violence is higher than in any other high income counties in the world.

<u>**Sandy Hook Elementary School Shooting**</u>

<u>**December 14th, 2012 *******</u>
Newtown, Connecticut

2 weeks before Christmas a young man killed his mother with her .<u>**22 caliber Savage MK 11-f rifle.**</u>
He then took her <u>**bushmaster xm15-e2s rifle**</u> to Sandy Hook Elementary School and entered 2 classrooms killing 15 of the 16 students in the first class and 5 of the 16 in the next class along with their teacher. All the children were in the 1st grade. Some of the children had been shot as many as 11 times.
 The shooter died from what appeared to be suicide.
President Obama traveled to the town to meet with the families of those killed.
This became the deadliest shooting at a grade school or high school in the history of America at the time.
Still there were more mass school shootings to come.

June 7th, 2013
Santa Monica, California
Santa Monica, College

A 23 year old built his own .223 caliber assault rifle and used it to kill his father and brother. Then he set the house on fire. He carjacked a woman making her drive to the college library. Along the way he shot and wounded a woman who tried to help, fired rounds at a city bus and a police cruiser.
He shot and wounded 3 in the college parking lot then was killed by police in the college library.
There was a note expressing regret for killing his family members.

October 21st, 2013
Sparks, Nevada
Sparks Middle School

A 12 year old with a <u>**semi automatic handgun**</u> killed a teacher and wounded 2 students before committing suicide. The gun had been kept above the refrigerator in an unlocked case.

December 13th, 2013
Centennial, Colorado
Arapahoe High School

Student killed another student then himself.

Chapter 2
<u>February 14th, 2018</u>

History of a gun

Parkland, Florida, Las Vegas Nevada, Sutherland Springs, Texas, all places in the news. What do they have in common? Mass shootings carried out with an **AR-15 rifle.**

In the mid 50's the army asked a gun company called Armalite to develop a smaller version **of the AR-10 to replace the M-1 Garland used in World War 2. They developed the AR-15.**

The design was eventually sold to Colt who began selling to Pentagon.

 In 1962 the U. S. Dept of Defense changed the name from AR-15 to M-16.

In 1963 Colt started marketing the AR-15 to the American public as a "Superb hunting partner."

In 1986 the Firearm Owners Protection Act banned NEW automatic weapons. The 1st Colt AR-15 was a semi automatic. Civilians own automatics grandfathered in before 1986.

In 1994 there was a Federal Assault weapons ban but it was allowed to expire in 2004. It banned 18 kinds of firearms including the AK-47 and the AR-15 but did not ban all semi-automatic weapons.

Parkland, Florida

In Florida before February 14th, 2018 Anyone older than 18, with a clean record could buy an AR-15 with **NO WAITING PERIOD.**

The State of California has recently banned all assault weapons including the AR-15.

Another School Shooting

On February 14th, 2018 a young man 19 years old entered Marjory Stoneman Douglas High School Building 12 and began shooting. When he was finished 17 lives had come to an end and 14 more were wounded. Some reports say the shooting started outside of the building then continued inside after a fire alarm went off. As the students left the classrooms the shooter opened fired. He dropped his weapon and hid within the crowd being evacuated after he quit shooting.

At 2:50 p. m. he went into a Wal- Mart and got a drink at the Subway inside.

At 2:53 p. m. deputies responded to the reports of a shooting at the school.

At 3:01 p. m. the shooter went inside a McDonald's where he stayed for awhile then left.

At 3:41 p. m. he was finally caught.

Thursday February 15th,2018

The shooter appeared in court and was ordered held without bail.

Friday February 16th, 2018

President Trump and his wife visited victims at Broward Health North Hospital.

Monday February 19th, 2018

There was a hearing at a Fort Lauderdale court.

Wednesday February 21st,2018

Broward County Sheriff says " qualified and trained " deputies will now carry rifles including AR-15 on campus to protect school students.

Thursday February 22nd,2018

School Resource Deputy is suspended pending an investigation. He then resigned and retired. It was reported he stayed outside the building during the shooting.

Saturday February 24th, 2018
It is now being reported at least 3 deputies waited outside while shooting was taking place.
Wednesday February 28th, 2018
The school reopened.

Thursday February 15th, 2018
In South Carolina a student was arrested after posting a threat on social media "Round 2 of Florida shooting tomorrow."

There have been at least 25 fatal school shootings in the United States since the 1999 Columbine shooting. It is no longer considered one of the 10 most deadliest shootings in American history. The shooting that took place February 14th, 2018 is reported to be the 18th shooting of the new year. It is also now among the 10 most deadliest mass school shootings.

The April 2007 Virginia Tech massacre led to NICS Improvement Act of 2007 to address loopholes in background checks when buying a gun.

December 2016
Social Security Administration issued a rule complying with the 2007 Act by submitting to NICS the names of people receiving disability checks that had a representative payee. The act ruled that people not mentally competent to handle their own money or hold full time employment should not be able to purchase firearms.

Federal agencies about disability opposed the rule on grounds that it promoted harmful stereotypes about people with disabilities.

In early 2017 Congress used Congressional Review Act to revoke the rule. It was the House Judiciary Resolution 40.

March 2017
Congress passed bill forbidding Dept of Veterans Affairs from submitting records to NICS.

<u>A bill introducing a ban on AR-15 style assault rifles was not even allowed a hearing.</u>

February14th 2018
Red Flags Ignored
<u>**Could this Shooting have been Prevented?**</u>

In the days after the terrible tragedy in Florida stories have surfaced about the numerous warnings that were ignored or not taken seriously enough. In **September 2017** there was a video on You Tube that the shooter made about school shootings. He reportedly said"I'm going to be a school shooter." He had been expelled from school and made threats towards other students. He was depressed after the death of his mother and was living with a friend.

In 2016 Florida Department of Children & Families investigated the boy as an alleged victim of medical neglect and inadequate supervision after a video was posted of him cutting his arms. They found him to be stable, not mistreated by his mother and receiving adequate care from a mental health counselor. At that time he was attending school.

The Sheriff's Office had received at least 20 calls about the suspect in the Florida mass shooting during the past few years.

January 5th, 2018 the <u>**FBI**</u> tip line was called about the boy "having a desire to kill" and "access to guns." Agents failed to investigate. The Florida Governor has called for the <u>**FBI**</u> director to resign.

The kids at school that knew him knew he was troubled and tried to warn those in authority but those warnings were not heeded.

It is because of the failure of those that received reports or stood outside the day of the shooting that 17 lives were lost including the School's Assistant Football coach who died a hero protecting students. Will things finally change?

Chapter 3
Federal Gun Laws

<u>Facts</u>

President Reagan-**11 mass murders**
President George H. W. Bush-**12 mass murders**
President Bill Clinton-**23 mass murders**
President George W. Bush-**20 mass murders**
President Obama-**162 mass murders**

Worst School Shootings

1. **April 20, 1999-Columbine High School-Colorado**
2. **April 16, 2007-Virginia Tech-   Virginia**
3. **December 14, 2012- Sandy Hook Elementary- Connecticut**
4. **February 14, 2018- Stoneman Thomas High- Florida**

Second Amendment:
This amendment protects the rights of citizens to "**to keep and bear arms.**

<u>**Major Federal Gun Laws**</u>

1. <u>**1934**</u> **National firearms Act: All Title 2 weapons such as machine guns, shotguns and short barreled rifles must be registered. The transfer and manufacture of such weapons is taxed.**
2. **1938 National Firearms Act: All person who import, manufacture, or sell firearms must have a Federal Firearms License. Certain classes of people (such as felons) are forbidden to own firearms.**
3. **Omnibus Crime Control and Safe Streets Act of 1968:Forbids trade between states for handguns. Age raised to 21 for buying handguns.**
4. **Gun control Act of 1968: Licensed manufacturers, dealers and importers are the only ones allowed to conduct interstate firearms transfers.**
5. **Firearm Owners Protection act(1986): Revised the Gun Control Act of 1968. Forbids the sale to civilians of** <u>**Automatic firearms made after the date of the law's passage.**</u>
6. **Gun Free School Zones Act 1990**
7. **Brady Handgun Violence Prevention Act 1993: Requires background checks on most people who buy a firearm.**
8. **Federal Assault Weapons Ban 1994- 2004: Banned Semiautomatics that looked like assault weapons.**
9. **Protection of Lawful Commerce in Arms Act 2005: Protects firearms manufacturers and licensed dealers from being held responsible for negligence when crimes are committed with their products.**

2 United States Supreme Court Cases:

2008-District of Columbia versus Heller:
The courts decision overturned a ban on handguns in the Federal District of Columbia. The majority opinion was that the **2nd Amendment protects the right of law abiding citizens to protect the defense of their homes with arms.**

 It was also stated that the 2nd Amendment is not an unlimited right. It doesn't give the right to carry a weapon for whatever purpose. Concealed weapons have been prohibited in some states and that has been upheld under the 2nd Amendment. There are prohibitions on possession of firearms by the <u>mentally ill or convicted felons.</u>

There are laws forbidding firearms being carried in <u>Schools or Federal Buildings.</u>

There are laws stating <u>Conditions & Qualifications on the Commercial Sale of Firearms.</u>

<u>2010</u>
McDonald Versus City of Chicago:

Court ruled due to the <u>Bill of Rights</u> The right of an individual to bear arms applies to not only Federal laws but also to State and local gun laws.

With all these laws why then have there been so many school shootings happening?

Eligible To Own Firearms:(There are other restrictions)

A United States Citizen
B. Permanent Resident Aliens
C. Non -Immigrant Aliens admitted to the country for lawful hunting or sporting purposes or if they are classified under an exception such as:

1. They have a valid hunting license issued by any U. S. State.
2. An official representative of a Foreign Government.
3. A distinguished Foreign Visitor recognized by the Department of State.
4. Someone with a waiver from the Attorney General as long as the waiver shows this would not endanger the public"s safety and would be in the interest of justice.

Manufacturers:
The law of the United States requires that anyone that has a business making guns or gun parts, or modifying guns to be resold **must be licensed as a manufacturer of firearms.**

c
Chapter 4
State Gun Laws

Federal gun laws, state gun laws, so many laws yet mass gun shootings especially school shootings continue to happen. Each state has its own set of gun laws. Just what are they?

A "shall issue state":

A state that has certain requirements for concealed weapons carry. The person should be a resident, be of a certain age, have their fingerprints taken and a background check run, attend a certified safety class and pass a hand gun proficiency test.

Each States Gun Laws

Alabama:(a state on list of states with most gun violence.)
1. **No permit needed to buy.**
2. **Not Required to register firearms.**
3. **No owner license required.**
4. **Handgun concealed carry permit required if in a vehicle.**
5. **No assault weapon laws.**

No background checks required for private sales.

Alaska:(a state on list of states with most gun violence.)
1. **No permit needed to buy.**
2. **Not required to register firearms.**
3. **No owner license required.**
4. **No concealed carry permit needed.**
5. **No assault weapon laws.**
6. **No background checks required for private sales.**
7. **All firearms must be certified within 30 days.**

Arizona(a state on list of states with most gun violence.)
1. **No permit needed to buy.**
2. **Not required to register firearms.**
3. **No owner license required.**
4. **No concealed carry weapon permit needed.**
5. **No assault weapon laws.**
6. **No background checks required for private sales.**
7. **All firearms must be certified within 60 days.**

Arkansas:(a state on list of states with most gun violence.)
1. **No permit needed to buy.**
2. **Not required to register firearms.**
3. **No owner license required.**
4. **No concealed carry weapon permit needed.**
5. **No background checks required for private sales.**

California
1. Permit needed to buy & must be through a dealer.
2. Registration required.
3. All firearms from other states should be reported to Department of Justice.
4. No owner license required
5. Assault weapons laws exist
6. Concealed carry laws exist.
7. Castle Doctrine Laws exist-State recognizes a legal presumption that an intruder poses a deadly threat.
8. Automatic weapons prohibited without a Department Of Justice "Dangerous Weapon Permit."
9.10 day waiting period for all private sales, firearms purchases and transfers.
10. Background checks for private transfers must be conducted by a licensed dealer who must keep a record of the sale as required by Federal Laws.

Colorado:
1. No permit to buy needed.
2. No registration required.
3. Denver bans assault weapons.
4. No owner license required.
5. Concealed carry weapons permit required for handguns.
6. Guns open carry allowed without a permit except in Denver and other areas with signs posted.
7. State Laws overrule city ordinances but Denver bans open carry and assault weapons.
8. Legal resident has right to defend home and property with a firearm.
9. Seller must have licensed dealer perform background check of buyer and the transfer must be approved by Colorado Bureau Of Investigation for private sells of firearms.

Connecticut:
1. Applicants for a Certificate of Eligibility must complete an approved safety course, pass a NICS background check as well as mental health records check. The certificate is for 5 years. There is a 14 day waiting period.
2. Registration required for assault weapons bought between September 13, 1994 and April 1, 2014 and machine guns bought before January 1, 2014.
3. Partial ban on selective firearms.
4. No owner permit required.
5. Concealed carry permits required.
6. Licensed open carry state.
7. Right to defend home and property with firearms.
8. Federal laws observed when traveling with a firearm.
9. Background check of the buyer required for private sales.

Delaware:
1. No State permit needed to buy firearms.
2. No registration required.
3. No assault weapon law.
4. No owner license required.
5. Concealed carry permits issued to those not barred from owning a firearms.
6. Open carry permitted.
7. Federal Laws observed when traveling.
8. Private sales background checks must be through licensed dealer.

District of Columbia:
1. The registration of firearms also serves as the permitting process. A background check and online training must be done and the registration is done through the Metropolitan Police Department.
2. Assault weapons banned.
3. Owner license same as registration process.
4. Open carry not allowed.
5. Short barreled shotguns and rifles, automatic firearms, and silencers not allowed.
6. Federal law for traveling with firearms.
7. Private gun sales must be done by licensed dealers.

Florida: (before February 14, 2018)
1. No state license needed.
2. No registration required.
3. No owner license required.
4. No assault weapon laws.
5. Concealed weapons permitted except long guns or machine guns.
6. No open carry allowed.
7. Making, throwing, discharging any destructive device is a <u>Felony.</u>
8. Federal law observed when traveling.
9. No background checks for private sales required.

Georgia: a state on list of states with most gun violence.
1. No permit needed to buy firearms.
2. No registration needed.
3. No assault laws.
4. No owner license required.
5. Concealed carry for handguns allowed with permit.
6. Open Carry allowed with license.
7. Federal laws observed when traveling.
8. No background checks for private sales.

Hawaii:
1. State permit required to buy firearms.
2. Registration requested within 5 days with county police chief or arriving in state.
3. Assault Weapons banned.
4. Owner does not need license but all firearms must be registered.
5. Concealed carry - State may issue permit but seldom does.
6. Hawaii is a licensed open carry state but seldom issues licenses.
7. Short barreled shotguns & rifles, machine guns are not allowed.
8. Federal laws observed when traveling.
9. Background check required for a permit to purchase a firearm.

Idaho:
1. No state permit needed to buy firearms.
2. No firearm registration needed.
3. No assault weapon law.
4. No owner license needed.
5. Carrying Concealed weapons allowed outside city limits and inside vehicles. Starting July 2018, within city is legal as long as Idaho resident and21 or older. If not a resident of state a permit is needed.
6. Cities may have laws about the use of firearms within their limits.
7. Federal laws observed when traveling.
8. No background checks for private sales.

Illinois:
1. To purchase a gun must have a Firearms Owners ID Card issued by State Police after a NICS background check, a Department of Human Services check. No Felons or persons convicted of assault or battery or domestic violence or anyone that is a subject of a protection order can be issued such card. The Department of Human Services keeps records of mentally defective or people that have been hospitalized within the last 5 years. They will not be issued a card to own a firearm. Cards issued before June 2018 are only good for 5 years. Cards after that date will be good for 10 years.
2. To own a firearm must have a Firearms Owners ID card.
3. No registration required.
4. Concealed Carry license issued by State Police.
5. No open carry of firearms allowed.
6. Must have concealed carry license to have firearms in vehicles.
7. City of Chicago and Cook County have banned having assault weapons.
8. A Federal Firearms License is required to sell firearms and the person must verify a valid F. O. I. D. card with the state police for the buyer.

Indiana:
1. No permit to purchase needed.
2. No firearm registration needed.
3. No assault weapon law.
4. No owner license needed.
5. "License to carry handgun" needed and covers concealed and open carry. As of July 17,2017 a person at least 18, who is protected by a protection order and has applied for a license may carry a handgun without a license for 60 days from the issue of the protection order.
6. License must be owned to carry in a vehicle.
7. Firearms must be certified within 15 days of ownership.
8. Federal laws observed when traveling.
9. Allowed to protect home and property when necessary.
10. No law to inform Law Enforcement of having a firearm.
11. No background checks required for private sale of guns.

Iowa:
1. Handguns require "permit to carry or permit to acquire" when being bought.
2. . Iowa is a "Shall Issue" state."Permit to Carry Weapons" is needed for open or concealed carrying of firearms.
3. Defense of home or property is allowed.
4. Registration not required
5.No assault weapons laws.
6.No owner license needed.
7.Machine guns are illegal as are destructive devices. Short barreled rifles and shotguns became legal April 13, 2017.
8. Private sales require a yearly "Permit to Acquire" or a "Permit To Carry."

Kansas:

1. No state permit needed to buy a firearm.
2. No registration needed.
3. No assault weapons law.
4. No owner license required.
5. No concealed carry permits required.
6. Short barreled machine guns and shotguns must be registered under the National Firearms Act.
7. Firearms must be certified within 15 days.
8. Federal rules observed when traveling.
9. No background checks required for private sales.

Kentucky:
1. Concealed weapons permit required.

2. Firearms must be certified within 15 days.
3. Secondary educational schools and government buildings can restrict concealed carry.
4. No other laws.

Louisiana:(state is listed on states with most gun violence list.)
1. State is a "shall issue" state for concealed carry.
2. No permit to buy required.
3. No registration required.
4. No owner license required.
5. No assault weapons laws.

Maine:
1. This state is a "shall issue " state for concealed carry.
2. Open carry is allowed.
3. City government may have restrictions on the firing of firearms.
4. Firearms must be certified within 15 days.

Maryland:
1. Training, fingerprints, background checks are required for a Handgun Qualification license to buy any handguns.
2. Automatic weapons must be registered. State police keep permanent records of handgun transfers.
3. Maryland is a "Shall Issue" state for concealed carry. Applicants must show a good reason for carrying a handgun.
4. Open carry is allowed with a carry license but seldom practiced.
5. Certain models of firearms are banned as assault pistols or long guns. It is not legal to have an assault weapon unless it was owned before October 1, 2013.
6. Federal law is observed for automatic firearms.
7. Private sales must go through a licensed dealer for handguns or assault weapons which means a background check on the buyer.

Massachusetts:
1. Firearm I. D. or license to carry required to buy firearms.
2. Transfer of firearms have to be recorded with the State Executive Office of Public safety and Security by the seller if in the state and by the buyer if out of the state. There is an option to register.
3. Firearm I. D. or license to carry required to own guns.
4. Massachusetts is a "May Issue" State for Concealed carry.
5. To open carry a person must have a Class a unrestricted license to carry. If Police ask to see the permit it must be shown.
6. A 2 point "banned features" defines assault weapons. They are unlawful unless legally owned before September 13, 1994.
7. Machine guns require a license.

Michigan:
1. Permit to buy required if the transaction is not through a dealer with a Federal Firearms License.
2. Sales of handguns must be registered with local law enforcement.
3. Owner is not required to have license.
4. State is a "May Issue state."
5. To carry firearms in a vehicle person must have a license. Open carry is allowed.
6. Private sales require the buyer to have 1 of the 2 licenses available.

Minnesota:
1. Permit to buy or permit to carry needed to buy handguns from F. F. license Dealers. Private seller regulations exist.
2. Firearms do not have to be registered.
3. Must be 18 with a permit to purchase in order to buy assault weapons. Permits to carry require you be 21 or older.
4. Owner license not required.
5. Minnesota is a "Shall Issue" state. Permit to carry needed for concealed weapons.
6. BB guns, rifles or shotguns in a public place is a gross misdemeanor. If you are under 21 with a semiautomatic assault weapon in public that is a felony.
7. Any legal firearm can be carried in a vehicle unloaded and in a case.
8. It is a gross misdemeanor if a private sell is made to a person not allowed to own a gun if a felony crime is committed with the first year of the sale.

Mississippi:(on list of most violent states)
1. No license to buy required.
2. No registration required.
3. No assault weapons law.
4. No owner license required.
5. No concealed carry license required if carried in a purse, handbag, briefcase etc.

No background checks for private sales.

Missouri:(on list of most violent states.)
1. Missouri is a "Shall Issue" state.
2. No assault weapons law.
3. Open carry is allowed.
4. No background checks for private sales required.

Montana:
1. No state permit needed to buy firearm.
2. No firearm registration needed.
3. No assault weapons laws.
4. No Owner License required.

Montana continued:

5. Concealed weapons permits issued for lawful residents at least 18.

6.Open carry allowed without license.

7. Cities may have laws for the possession of firearms by Felons, Minors, Illegal Aliens, or Mentally Incompetent.

8. There is a Universal background check ordinance put in place in 2016 for private sales. However the Attorney General declared it unlawful.

Nebraska:
1. A handgun certificate or concealed carry permit is needed to buy handguns.
2. City of Omaha registers all handguns. City of Lincoln requires reporting of all firearm sales.
3. No owner license required.
4. Nebraska is a "Shall Issue" state for concealed carry.
5. Open Carry is allowed with some exceptions.
6. Vehicle firearms must be in sight.
7. No Assault Weapons law.
8. All private sales of Handguns must have certificate or permit therefore must have had background checks.

Nevada:
1. No permit needed to buy firearms.
2. No firearms registration required.
3. No owner license needed.
4. Nevada is a "shall issue" state for concealed carrying.
5. Open carry is allowed.
6. In a vehicle firearm may be anywhere except carried upon a person unless they have concealed carry permit.
7. Cities may have laws about the firing of firearms.
8. No Assault Weapons law.
9. Having any N F A items is subject to Federal Laws.
10. On November 16, 2016 voters approved background checks for private sales.

New Hampshire:
1. No State permit needed to buy firearms.
2. No registration needed.
3. No Assault Weapons law.
4. No ownership license needed.
5. Open carry is allowed without permit.
6. Loaded long guns not allowed in vehicles.
7. No travel laws.
8. No background checks for private sales.

New Jersey:
1. To buy a shotgun or rifle or handgun ammunition a lifetime purchaser I. D. card is needed. To buy a handgun a Permit to purchase Permit is required. This permit is good for 90 days. Only 1 handgun can be bought within a 30 day time frame. The permits or I. D. cards are supposed to be given on a "Shall Issue" basis but authorities often want applicants to justify their need of a handgun.
2. New Jersey Police Firearms Investigation Unit keeps records of all handguns transfers with some exceptions. New Jersey residents buying firearms must buy from a licensed dealer in the state or private resident of the state. a copy of the purchase permit is sent to NJPFIU.
3. Owner license for owning any firearm is required. Machine guns are not legal.
4. New Jersey does not issue concealed carry or open carry permits. There are some exceptions.
5. Assault firearms owned before May 1990 and registered with the state are legal to own. After that date assault weapons are not legal to own.
6. Machine Guns require a State license and are next to impossible to obtain.

New Mexico:
1. No permit to own needed.
2. No registration needed.
3. No assault weapon laws.
4. No owner license needed.
5. To acquire a concealed carry permit you must hold a valid new Mexico I. D. or driver's license. You must be a full time or part time resident. you must pass a criminal background check, mental health records check, and complete a 15 hour handgun safety course. some are exempt from the training requirements. concealed carrying unlawfully is a petty misdemeanor punished by up to 6 months in jail and a fine up to $500.
6. Open carry of a rifle or handgun is legal without a permit.
7. Carrying of a firearm in a vehicle without a permit is legal.
8. New Mexico recognizes permits from 24 other states.
9. Using a firearm in the home must be in self-defense only. Lethal force defending property is not justified.
10. Native American Reservations may recognize state laws while some have more restrictive laws.
11. No background checks for private sales required. Criminal trespassing is a misdemeanor punishable by less than 1 year in jail and /or fine up to $1,000.

New York:
1. No permit needed for long guns outside of New York City. Handgun permits for purchase are issued by County or Supreme court judges and require a background check. The exceptions are New York City, Nassau and Suffolk Counties.
2. All handguns must be registered under a license. handguns are registered with a purchase permit. Any unregistered firearm is not legal. All rifles classified as assault weapons must be state registered. New York City has different laws.

New York continued:

      3. Ownership of handguns needs to be licensed. There are 3 types of licenses. A Person must be 21 or older. These licenses are not legal in New York City.

      4.Concealed Carry licenses issued by New York State Counties and some Police Departments. Concealed Carrying of a loaded weapon without a permit is considered a felony. To be considered a legal permit in New York City, it must be validated by the Police Commissioner.

      5. Assault weapons are banned with exceptions of those legally owned on January 2013 and registered with the state. New York City, Albany, Rochester and Buffalo are cities with their own assault weapons ban.

      6. Title 2 National Firearms Act is recognized in New York State.

      7. Defense of home and person is allowed.

      8. For private sales a licensed dealer must do a background check, provide documentation of the check to the state police and keep a record of sale.

      9. Some cities within the state have more restrictive gun laws such as New York City.

North Carolina:

1. A Pistol Purchase or Concealed Handgun Permit is needed to buy a handgun.
2. Firearms do not need to be registered.
3. No ownership license is required.
4. North Carolina is one of the "shall issue" states. A law enforcement officer must be informed if they confront a person with a concealed firearm.
5. State laws override city laws regarding gun laws.
6. Title 2 firearms must meet Federal rules.
7. No Assault weapons law.
8. Firearms must be certified within 15 days.
9. 2 permits require background checks and a person must have a permit for private sales.

North Dakota:

1. No permit needed to buy firearms.
2. No registration needed.
3. No ownership license required.
4. North Dakota is a "shall issue" state for concealed carry. As of August 2017, a permit is no longer needed for concealed carry.
5. Open carry needs legal concealed carry permit.
6. No Assault Weapon laws.
7. N F A compliant. <u>Automatic Firearms </u>must be registered with County Sheriff as well as State Bureau of Criminal Investigation.
8. Owners of firearms have 30 days to get them certified.
9. No background checks needed for private sales.

Ohio:
1. No permit needed to buy.
2. No registration needed.
3. No Assault Weapons law.
4. No owner license needed.
5. For Concealed Carry, 8 hours of training required. Ohio is a "shall issue" state.
6. For Open carry a person must be 18 or older to carry a firearm without a permit.
7. There are restrictions for having a firearm in a motor vehicle or licensed liquor businesses.
8. N F A firearms legal if registered according to N F A laws.
9. Firearms must be certified within 45 days.
10. Observation of Federal Laws required when traveling with a firearm.
11. Ohio is a "Duty to Inform" state. If approached by a law enforcement officer must let them know if you have a firearm.
12. Private Sales do not require a background check.

Oklahoma:
1. No permit to buy needed.
2. Private Sales are legal with NO waiting period.
3. No registration needed.
4. No ownership license needed.
5. Concealed Carry allowed.
6. Open carry is allowed with a permit as of November2012. Must have handgun license.
7. Firearms must be certified within 15 days.
8. <u>Short barreled rifles and shotguns must be registered under N F A laws.</u>
9. <u>Automatic Firearms are legal.</u>
10. No background checks needed for private sales.

Oregon:
1. No permit needed to buy.
2. Oregon State Police maintain records of firearm sales from F F L dealers and holds them for 5 years.
3. No Assault Weapons law.
4. No license for ownership required.
5. For residents Oregon is a "shall issue" state.
6. Open Carry is legal.
7. Traveling with a firearm is regulated under <u>Federal Law "Title 18."</u>
8. Private Sales must be by licensed firearm dealer. They do background check and keep a record of the sale.
9. Red Flag Law* A court may be petitioned for a 1- year order making it illegal for a person to have deadly weapons if they are considered a danger to themselves or others.

Pennsylvania:
1. No permit needed to buy.
2. Handgun buyers have a P I C S check done during time of sale. A Record is kept in the State Police "Sales Data Base."By doing a P I C S check a background check is completed.
3. No Assault Weapon laws.
4. No ownership license needed.
5. Pennsylvania is a "shall issue" state. L T C F required for concealed carry on one's person, in a vehicle or during a state of emergency.
6. Unlicensed open carry exception: Not allowed in City of Philadelphia or vehicles.
7. Firearms used in protection of home is allowed. Outside of the home it must be a clear case of self-protection and not fatal.
8. Private Sales must be through licensed dealer or at a county sheriff's office. Background checks will be done.

Rhode Island:
1. The Rhode Island Department of Environmental Management issues a "blue card" after buyer passes a safety exam.
2. No registration needed.
3. No Assault Weapons law.
4. No owner license needed but "blue card" is.
5. Rhode Island is a "shall issue" state. Local authorities were deferring applicants to the Attorney General. In April 2015 Rhode Island Supreme Court ruled police chiefs must accept and review applications and must give a decision. They must show cause when denying an application.
6. Handgun owners must have a carry permit for handguns in a vehicle. Out of state permits for vehicles only are recognized.
7. Right to protect home is allowed.
8. N F A weapons are restricted.
9. Traveling with a handgun is allowed as long as there are no unnecessary stops. Non-residents must have carry permit from another state for handguns.
10. All sales of handguns even private sales must have background checks.
11. No Red Flag Laws* In 2018 the Governor signed an order stating "No additional authority is given to law enforcement officers to seize guns from a person."

South Carolina:
1. No permit needed to buy.
2. No registration needed.
3. No ownership license needed.
4. South Carolina is a "shall issue" state.
5. No Open Carry of handguns.
6. No Assault Weapons law.
7. For travel Federal Laws are observed.
8. No background checks required for private sales.

South Dakota:
1. No permit needed to buy firearms.
2. No registration needed.
3. No ownership license needed.
4. South Dakota is a "shall issue" state for concealed carry.
5. Open carry is allowed.
6. If carrying a firearm in a vehicle it must be seen.
7. No Assault Weapon law.
8. No background checks required for private sales.

Tennessee:
1. No permit needed to buy
2. No registration needed.
3. No assault weapon law.
4. No ownership license needed.
5. Permits for Concealed Carry are "shall issue."
6. Open carry allowed with a permit.
7. as of July 2014 handguns are allowed in vehicles without a permit.
8. As of July 2017 handguns bought legally can be carried by owners of a protection order for 60 days without a license.
9. Loaded long guns being carried in public are illegal.
10. Firearms must be certified within 15 days.
11. Federal Laws observed for travel with firearms.
12. Self defense of home business or vehicle is allowed.
13. No background check needed for private sales.

Texas:
1. No permit needed to buy.
2. No registration needed.
3. No Assault weapon law.
4. No ownership license needed.
5. Texas is a "shall issue" state. Handguns Concealed Carry license can not be issued if the applicant is under 21, a convicted felon, a fugitive, a chemical dependent person, or owes child support or taxes.
6. Open Carry is allowed with a handgun license.
7. Concealed Carry on College Campus is allowed.
8. state Laws prohibits city from firearms laws except concerning the firing of firearms.
9. <u>Explosive weapons, machine guns, short barreled firearms, firearm silencers,</u> must be <u>Registered in</u> National Firearms & Transfer Records.
10. Protection of home and self is allowed.
11. No background checks needed for private sale of firearms.

Utah:
1. No permit needed to buy.
2. No registration needed.
3. No Assault Weapon laws.
4. No ownership license needed.
5. Concealed carry is allowed with a permit.
6. Open carrying of unloaded firearms is allowed without permit. Loaded must have permit.
7. firearms must be certified within 15 days.
8. Defending home and self is allowed.
9. No background check needed for private sales.

Vermont:
1. Concealed Carry or Open Carry without permit is allowed if a citizen or lawful admitted alien.
2. Vermont made suppressors legal in 2015.
3. No license, permits ownership license, needed.
4. No assault weapons law.

Virginia:
1. no permit to buy needed.
2. No ownership license needed.
3. Machine guns must be registered with State Police.
4. Proof of Age & citizenship needed for buying Assault weapons.
5. A "shall issue" state for Concealed Carry.
6. Non-residents can be issued permits. Training is allowed to be done online or in person for permit.
7. Must be 18 or older for Open Carry.
8. Several cities Do Not Allow Open Carry of assault weapons, or shotguns that have a magazine that holds more then 5 rounds of ammunition. A permit is needed in these cities. Cities of: Alexandria, Chesapeake, Fairfax, Falls Church, Norfork Newport News, Richmond, Virginia Beach.
9. Open Carry in vehicles must be secured in glove box, center console or trunk.
10. Assault weapons require Proof of Age-18 for long guns, 21 for pistols and Proof of Citizenship.
11. Machine guns must be registered with State Police.
12. Private sales do not require background checks.

Washington:
1. No state permit to buy needed.
2. Retail Dealers must record and report all retail sales to <u>local police or sheriff </u>and to <u>State Department of Licensing.</u>
3. No ownership license needed.
4. Washington Constitution has "Right to Bear Arms."
5. Concealed Carry: Washington is a "shall issue" state.
6. Open Carry is legal.
7. In vehicles loaded shotguns only allowed with a concealed Carry Pistol Permit.
8. No Ban on Assault Weapons.
9. Machine guns are Not Legal unless purchased before July 1994.
10. Travel subject to Federal Laws.
11. Allowed to protect in the home by using a firearm.
12. Private Sales require a licensed dealer, background check, and record of sale.
13. Red Flag Law * Police may temporarily take guns if a judge finds a person a threat to themselves or others.

West Virginia:
1. No permit to buy needed.
2. No registration needed.
3. No ownership license needed.
4. as of may 2016 Concealed Carry requires a person is 21 or older and Legally able to own a firearm in order to carry without a permit. 18 to 20 needs a permit. West Virginia is a "shall issue" state.
5. As of October 2016, 37 states recognize WV permits for persons 21 or older. 16 states recognize WV permits for person 18 to 20 years of age.
6. Open Carry does not need a permit.
7. No Assault weapons law.
8. Firearms must be certified within 30 days.
9. Private sales do not require background checks.

Wisconsin:
1. Constitutional "Right To Bear Arms."
2. No permit to buy needed.
3. Wisconsin is a "shall issue" state for Concealed Carry.
4. No ownership license needed.
5. Open Carry does not need permit for firearms or knives.
6. Self defense is allowed for home or business however deadly force is not allowed when defending property.
7. No registration needed.
8. No assault Weapons law.
9. Private Sales do not require background checks.

Wyoming:
1. No permit to buy needed.
2. No registration required.
3. No Assault weapons law.
4. No ownership license needed.
5. concealed carry or Open Carry do not require permits.
6. Wyoming is a "shall issue " state for residents who want a permit.
7. N F a weapons are not restricted.
8. Background checks for private sales are not required.

Notes about State Laws.
1. They cover the sales, possession and use of firearms as well as ammunition.
2. Each state has its own laws regarding firearms.
3. State laws are in addition to federal firearm laws. Some states have stricter laws while some have more lenient ones.
4. State Constitutions have provisions like the Second amendment of the United States Constitution except for the states of: California, Maryland, New Jersey, Iowa, Minnesota and New York.
5. The protection of the 2nd amendment for self-defense in a persons home stands against state governments.
6. Some states do not recognize out of state permits for firearms.
7. State and city police are not legally commanded to enforce federal gun laws.
8. The facts presented were before 2018 School shooting in Florida. Some of the laws might have been changed or added to since then.

States and School shootings from 2010-2018

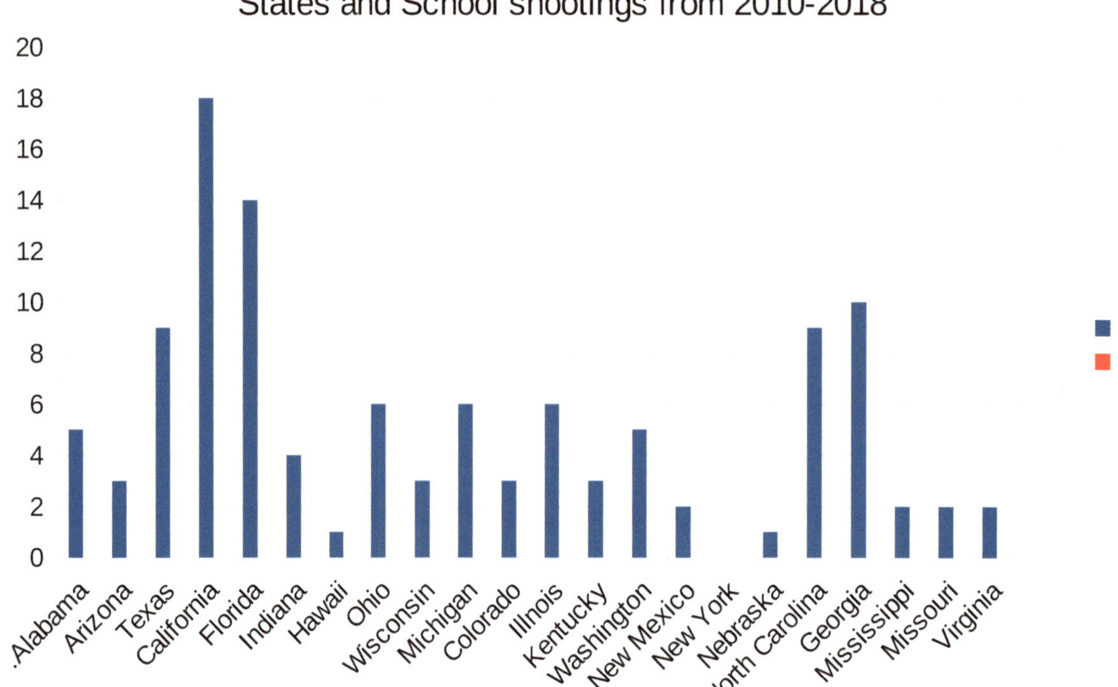

States and School Shooting Deaths Since 1996-2003

State	Year	Deaths
Washington	1996	3
Arkansas	1997	2
Mississippi	1997	2
Arkansas	1998	5
Pennsylvania	1998	1
Tennessee	1998	1
Oregon	1998	4
Colorado	1999	13
New Mexico	1999	1
Michigan	2000	1
Georgia	2000	2
Florida	2000	1
Maryland	2001	1
California	2001	2
Indiana	2001	1
Arizona	2002	3
Louisiana	2003	1
Pennsylvania	2003	1
Minnesota	2003	2

State	Year	Deaths
Minnesota	2005	9
Tennessee	2005	1
Vermont	2006	2
Colorado	2006	1
Wisconsin	2006	1
Pennsylvania	2006	5
Louisiana	2008	2
Virginia	2007	32
Illinois	2008	5
Florida	2008	1
Alabama	2010	1
Alabama	2010	3
Ohio	2010	2
Nebraska	2011	2
Texas	2011	1
Virginia	2011	1
Ohio	2012	3
Florida	2012	1
California	2012	7
Wisconsin	2012	6
Oregon	2012	2
California	2013	6
Washington	2014	5
Oregon	2015	6
California	2017	6
Connecticut	2017	3
Florida	2018	17

There have been 146 school shootings from 2000 to beginning of 2018.
There have been 158 deaths from school shooting from 2000 to beginning of 2018.
There have been 246 injuries in that time frame.

Chapter 5
Guns and politics

When America was young firearms were a necessary part of life. They were needed for hunting for food and for survival. Before the American Revolution there was a need for the militia due to a lack of manpower, or desire for keeping a full time army. During the early years of the country firearms were needed for protection as settlers moved west and exploration of America continued to add to its growth.

Gun control laws were attempted in 1813 in Kentucky when state law tried to stop the carrying of concealed weapons. That led to opposition and gun rights formed around the 2nd Amendment. The first State Court decision was in Kentucky in 1842 and it decided " the rights of citizens to bear arms in defense of themselves and the state must be preserved."

The 1st half of the 20th Century:

The United States Supreme Court has constantly ruled that the 2nd amendment did not restrict States from having and enforcing gun laws. A major Federal firearms law was passed in 1934.**The national Firearms Act made machine guns, short barreled rifles and shotguns under the jurisdiction of the Bureau of Alcohol, Tobacco, and Firearms.**

The 2nd half of the 20th Century:

After the assassinations of President John Kennedy, Martin Luther King Jr. and Robert Kennedy the <u>Gun Control Act of 1968</u> was passed. Interstate Firearm transfers must be done by licensed dealers, importers or manufacturers. There are certain types of people not allowed to buy firearms such as convicted felons.
After the murder of John Lennon and an assassination attempt on the president in 1981 the <u>Brady Handgun Violence Prevention Act of 1993</u> became law. It required a <u>National Background Check System</u> in hopes that it would keep restricted persons from buying or traveling with firearms.

A retired Supreme Court Justice made a comment about the difference between hunting 200 years ago and now. He noted it is no longer a necessary to survive but it is now sport. <u>Machine guns and Saturday Night Specials</u> are not sport firearms and there needs to be laws concerning them.

In 1986 <u>Congress</u> passed the <u>Firearms Owners Protection Act. It was supported by the N R A. It reversed</u> many of the laws of the 1968 Gun Control Act. It also made it necessary for the <u>purchase or sale of fully automatic rifles to be registered</u> and the firearm itself had to be registered.

<u>**In 1994 there was a Federal Assault Weapons Ban but it only lasted 10 years and was not renewed in 2004 by Congress. It banned the manufacture and transfer of semi-automatic weapons and large magazines for firearms.**</u>

The 21st Century:
In 2 Supreme Court cases it was ruled that the 2nd amendment protects a person's right of self-defense.

Political Arguments about Gun rights:

Going back to the early days of the foundation of America and 2nd Amendment rights it is sometimes argued that gun laws and the banning of guns enables government tyranny.
There are groups that oppose any and all gun laws. The Gun Owners Of America was started in 1975 after there was a proposal to ban all handguns in California. There is a group called the Second Amendment Foundation and one called Second Amendment Sisters. They do not believe in gun restrictions.

The *National Rifle Association* was started in 1871 to promote firearm competency. They supported the *National Firearms Act* and the *Gun Control Act.* They also supported the *Firearm Owners Protection Act.*
During the 1970's the NRA became politically active. By 1998 they were one of the biggest spenders in Elections for Congress.

The Brady Campaign To Prevent Gun Violence started in 1974 under a different name. The name was changed in 2001. It at one time contributed $75,000 to Campaigns for Congress.

In 1996 Congress while funding the Center For Disease Control and Prevention added language that did not allow any funds for injury prevention and control to be used to promote gun control.

The NRA opposed bans on handguns in several states. They did however support the N I C S Improvement Amendments Act of 2007.

Gun Advocacy Groups both for and against gun control spend Millions of dollars through Political Action committees and lobbying firms to affect elections.

Chapter 6
The World and School Shootings

Australia
A lone gunman killed 35 people in 1996. The Prime Minister banned automatic and semi-automatic firearms. The Australian Government bought back and destroyed an estimated 600,000 banned guns. Now almost completely free of mass shootings.

Germany
Finland
Scotland

There were Major policy changes in response to attacks on schools. The last decade school shootings have been at ZERO.

Switzerland:
Gun Ownership is high but there are NO school shootings. The background check takes a week. Authorities keep a list people feared to become school shooters.

Germany:
Anyone under 25 must pass a rigorous Mental and Medical Health Exam.
Teachers trained to deal with troubled students and get them help.

Epilogue

This book started with one single thought "Why are there so many school shootings now?"
Were there school shootings when I was growing up? I didn't think there were but doing
research I soon learned school shootings have a long history, back to the 1800's.

Working on this book took a long time, lots of research, note taking, reading and writing.
I have learned new things I didn't know. Some things I had learned in school but forgotten about.

There are Federal, State even City laws regarding firearms. There is a Federal Constitution and
there are State Constitutions also. So why are there so many School shootings?

In 2018 only 3 months old there have been at least 19 school shootings. The one in Florida
February 14th, was _Not_ the last one. While some states have added new laws such as Oregon
and Florida others have _Not._

Depending on which side you take there are numerous reasons for school shootings. The people
that swear by the 2nd amendment say its the kids, the social media, the video games, the movies
and television shows kids watch, the parents but never do they suggest it is the laws or lack of
them.

In 2018 after Parkland the school shooters brother was arrested for trespassing on the school
grounds. March 21st, 2018 2 students were arrested for carrying knives to school.

March 20th 2018 in Maryland there was another school shooting 2 wounded 1 killed. The
shooting was stopped by a guard at the school. The gun used belonged to the boys father and was
legal.

Today March 22 2018 the Governor of Florida has placed 8 State troopers at Parkland to help
secure entry points and keep students safe.
On Saturday March 24 2018 There will be a March on Washington by students from all over
America demanding change.

The right to bear arms is protected by the 2nd amendment but what about the right to life?
Why do students, parents, grandparents have to live in fear that a school shooting will end their
life or the life of a loved one?
In 1994 there was a federal ban on semi-automatic weapons being made or transferred but 10
years later it was allowed to end. _For those 10 years there was a drop in school shootings._

_Smart Guns only fire when in the hands of the owner yet they have not been allowed to be
developed and sold due to death threats and opposition._ Would that help keep kids at home from
picking up a gun and shooting a brother or sister by accident or even themselves? Wouldn't it
keep guns from being carried into schools and used to take innocent lives?

Hawaii has some of the most strictest gun laws. How many school shooting have occurred there?
<u>Only 1.</u>

<u>The state gun laws vary from state to state.</u>
That is to me a very big reason for what is happening in America today. The laws and the Constitutions go back to the beginning of our country's beginning and that is another reason we have school shootings.

There are a lot of things that could help end school shootings besides stricter gun laws but without better gun laws and gun law enforcement nothing we as parents, grandparents or students do will be enough.
Until Government and Citizens come together and work together to stop school shootings they will in all likelihood continue.

1. Why can kids get guns their parents have at home?
2. Why aren't private sales mandated to be done by a FFl dealer so that background checks are done?
3. Why doesn't every State have Red Flag laws?
4. Why aren't all firearm sales required to have records kept and background checks done?
5. Why aren't machine guns and Assault weapons banned in all 50 states?
6. Why aren't owners of firearms required to have a license in all 50 states?

References
No Copyright infringement is intended by notes taken regarding information from these sites.

1. www.statisticbrain.com
2. https//en.wikipendia.org/wiki/Gun politics in the United States
3. same   /concealed carry in U. S.
4. same   /gun laws by state
5. same   / gun laws in U. S.
6. www.rollingstone.com/school shootings since 2000
7. https//thinkprogress.org/a timeline of mass shootings since Columbine

If you have enjoyed this book you can find my other books on amazon.com under Ann Marie McKay. Below are some of the covers and titles. A review of this book would be appreciated.

Diary of A Fire

To You From Me Wherever You Are

I have over 35 books self published. Some are poetry, some are love stories. There are children's picture books and a few written about astrology. The first one in this series is What Happened To The America I Grew Up In? I sincerely hope you have enjoyed this book and found it interesting.

God bless
Annie